# This Woman
# Is Haunted

# This Woman
# Is Haunted

*poems*

Betsy Littrell

*atmosphere press*

Published by Atmosphere Press

Cover design by Senhor Tocas
Author photo by Melissa Alexander



This Woman is Haunted
2020, Betsy Littrell

atmospherepress.com

# Table of Contents

1

3 Otis Street..........3
Trailer Park After Dark.........5
Teen Spirit..........7
Unplugged..........8
Dirty Bath Water.........9
In the Form of Flowers..........10
Don't Send Me Flowers..........11


2

Morning Tea..........15
Unbending..........16
For Some Reason..........17
Bus Rider..........18
Combat Hunger..........19
In Line at Trader Joe's..........20
Memory..........21
From My Porch..........22
Afternoon Tea..........23
Swallow..........24
Row 12, Seat A..........25
Message: Undeliverable..........27
I don't feel like a lady..........28
Santa Barbara..........29
The Black Dress..........30
Why doesn't she have any wrinkles on her face?..........32
Evening Tea..........34

## 3

Moonless Mexico..........37
On Top of Crisp Sheets..........46
The Sweater..........47
Undone..........48
Copacetic..........49
I don't..........50
Christina's World..........51
Getting Dressed for the Ball..........52
I Couldn't Sleep..........53
Sunset.........54
On a Field, Sable, the Letter A, Gules..........55
The Dream..........56
Ode to Pain..........57

## 4

March 19, 2003..........61
Memory By Scent..........62
Lauren..........63
In His Own Room..........64
Crosswalk..........65
Soaking..........66
The Power of the Dragon..........67
Backwash..........68
Anxiety..........69
Mother Isn't Always Right..........70
Amen..........71

*For Joshua, Gabriel, Nicholas and Kellen*
*Dreams Do Come True*

My house is haunted.
Four bedrooms, three
baths, recently updated.
It doesn't look a thing like
the old mansion at 7th and A
where I can see the ghosts
just as clearly as I observe
dusty books on library shelves
when I peek in the windows.
My ghosts prefer to hide—
whether it's under my bed,
beneath a pile of colored sweaters,
or in the jewelry drawer in the closet. Everything
seems immaculate but sometimes
a shadow follows me only
to disappear when I look
over my left shoulder.
I keep secrets
but I stay quiet, so quiet that I
shake. I've thought about moving,
but *they* will move with me,
close to the secrets, buried
with the woman behind a darkened window.

# I

# 3 Otis Street

This house is yellow. It used to be bone white.
Yes, I lived here when I was a little
girl, hair down to my waist, always in braids.
You've lived here almost twenty years now,
so it's ok with me that you made some changes.
This old Victorian needed
to be brought back to life, a brighter one.

The foyer is as cold as I remember,
winter boots piled high, though none fit me now.
That's the closet where I used to hide
underneath my mom's puffy and woolen
jackets, feeling the wall for a secret
passage that didn't exist. I wanted to escape.
Did you try to find a way out, too?
I was sure this house was haunted,
all the creaks and squeaks and rattles,
all warning me of something — or someone.
We had the ugliest golden
carpet, matted and stained, and the green
paisley couches had matching arm protectors.
The dining room was always empty,
but I kept my crayons and coloring books
in these built-in shelves. The kitchen
is different, modern now. Mom hated to
cook in the old one, but maybe
she would like the stainless
steel appliances and
white granite countertops.

The crazy second staircase is still

here, just as narrow. My sister's
room was on the left. I can almost smell
the cedar bookshelf filled with Nancy Drew
mysteries and the Funk and Wagnall
encyclopedias. The windows
are original and drafty, heavy, letting the eerie
chill in. I see you didn't cut down
the giant maple. My dad, gone eight years now,
would rake the leaves into rounded red
and orange piles just so I could jump in. Did you ever
find the box of evil memories I buried
in the dirt, past where the garden used to be?
It was ugly and gray, storms locked
inside. I don't think I dug down deep enough.
Maybe the memories became tangled
in the canes of the raspberries.

Let's find my old room, it was next
to the attic. I see you changed
the wallpaper - it's painted a pale pink now.
My parents let me design this room,
and I wanted to be an astronaut. The walls
used to be pasted with red, blue and
yellow stars with a rocket border, and
I dreamed I could fly to the moon.

# Trailer Park After Dark

Trailer Park After Dark is not the bar on Fifth Avenue
of the same name, but the bipolar mood

of a hormonal teenage girl. At fifteen, I pounded
my fists and legs on the ground until the tears

started to flow. That was the year I first
took a drink. That first time was

with Kim, who bribed a man to buy us Icehouse and
Zima at a convenience store. She drove us

to the woods where we laughed hysterically and talked
about boys we liked. We pissed all over

the pinecones, dirt and weeds. Somehow we made it back
to the trailer she lived in. I was thirsty,

I mean sand-in-my-throat-thirsty. I chugged
half a bottle of cranberry juice and immediately

threw up all over the long t-shirt I had changed into
to sleep in while I stumbled over to the sink to finish

vomiting. It was Kim's shirt, and I felt bad
for the dark red stain I left on it.

She told me it was a good thing I threw up, that I'd
feel better in the morning because of it. I met my

parents in church the next morning, hungover but holding it

together. God judged me while I sang, cranberry vomit still on my breath.

# Teen Spirit

His mother caught his
stepfather bare-assed, on top
of another woman. So she
grabbed all of his
guns and threw them
in the river. The boy,
a teenage opportunist,
fished the guns
out of the river, bare-
handed, on a cool April
spring day, acid
washed jeans and
flannel shirt, soaking wet.
He skated to the local pawn shops,
only those with neon signs, selling
his stepfather's prized gear,
and when he had enough
money, he bought himself
his first guitar,
feeling stupid and contagious.

# Unplugged

His face twitched,
just muscle spasms,
his brain departed.

The room  smells
of cotton balls and stiff linen.
Breathe, I told myself,
because he couldn't.

Thinking of the gap between his teeth,
I stand by a strong mahogany casket,
lid closed, too many lilies,
one hand on my belly,
a kick inside of me.

# Dirty Bath Water

I don't remember what shirt I wore
the day I was supposed to be on the
other side of the hemisphere, but
I was eating ketchup  on saltines,
thinking about my Barbie coloring
book, my mother beside me at the
solid wood kitchen table, her picture
glowing, strokes smooth, while my
greens and blues bled over the
lines, my image rumpled. Naturally,
I missed my flight, so I climbed
into dirty bath water, scrubbing
my blemishes deeper
into my skin

# In the Form of Flowers

Mom bought me blonde-headed Barbies and
Cabbage Patch dolls dressed in lavender
and flowers, smelling of baby powder,
but she knew how to pile on the guilt
like weeks of unfolded laundry.

I dial her number, and I can picture
her in bed in a floral
nightgown when she says in her
Massachusetts accent, *I haven't heard
from you in a while.* And then she tells me,
legs dangling off her mattress,
that her grandchildren are growing
up without knowing her. I imagine her
running her fingers through her dyed-blonde hair,
*Why don't you come for a visit? It's been
too long.* This conversation answers
her questions in my mind.

Yes, she's getting older and can
never remember where she put
that birthday card she bought me, although
she does remember to complain
about my sister's haircut or to tell me Billy is divorced
again,
but I really must find a florist
and send her some carnations,
ruffled ones with pink edges.

# Don't Send Me Flowers

He surprised me with 17
red roses, my first flowers,
and all I could think
about was the cider beer
on his breath. I kissed him,
drunk on his spit, and hung
the thorny stems
upside down on the wall,
draped over thumb tacks,
scarlet with crinkled brown edges.

Weighing myself on his mother's
bathroom scale, I was pleased
when the needle settled on 95.
I starved myself for him.
Next time, I was 20,
white roses matching
the uniform he wore the day
he was commissioned
in the Navy, chest bare
of medals, just a black name tag
and a golden anchor
on his hat. Tightly curled blossoms
opened in a vase by the window,
petals falling before I could
preserve them.

A decade later, my dad
died and I was pregnant with sadness
and baby number three. The lilies, cocky
with their star-shaped petals

and yellow-tinged centers wildly exposed,
scratched my throat, and all I could think
about was how I went from sitting on Daddy's lap
in his beat up beige La-Z-Boy to
sitting in the funeral home
unable to cry. If I close my eyes,
I can still smell mahogany mixed with gladiolas—
and picture the plaque on his grave.

# 2

# Morning Tea

When I woke up, my hair
seemed a shade darker, perhaps
to match brown eyes. I remember how
I threw up after eating an apple and cheese,
pregnant with my second son. Why didn't
I update the album with new photographs? I
tossed the drooping white roses, tinged with
brown in cloudy water, but I didn't have it in me
to make the bed. I boiled water for my tea bag,
wishing it was wine, contemplated my
ghostly heart, locked myself in
the bathroom and cried into my tea.
I wondered if the tea would still soothe me with the
salty tears. I tasted it, but I didn't know. I didn't know.

# Unbending

Her fingers, long and lean—
a piano player's.

She finds her hands strumming
dark notes — adagio.

*This is who I am.*

The notes become wild, ferocious,
without giving her body warning — vivacissimo.

*That is who I am.*
She smells
blue in the air.

Fingers relax, unbending.

# For Some Reason

I told people I was born
in a gas station, the one
where pump #3 is always
broken. My eyes are the color
of the Wrigley's spearmint gum
package, found  in aisle #2 and also
by the cash register. I like being

39, but I don't know
if I want to be 40. Maybe
I'll drink a bottle
of wine in the rain instead.
I remember eating popsicles
in my flowered jumper. You,
you wanted red, but green,
a green so green, sour like
limes, was my favorite. Those days

I made mud pies while Robin
washed her car after a downpour. I wove
a crown of daisies, dirty after
rolling down the hill. I think I'll
braid another crown
before I go to check to see
if pump #3 works today. My money
is on no, and I hear
the fire truck's siren.

# Bus Rider

The man at the bus stop
startled me; it was late at night
and I was carrying a bag
of plums and lemons. *Hello*
he said in a voice, gritty
like sand, and I didn't know
if he was speaking to the towering
oak tree, the concrete
bench, the wooly stars or me,
but I decided to say hello back,
nodding my head, almost
recognizing his face
as one imprinted deep in the folds
of my brain, and I almost made
it through a full day without thinking
of his possum-tailed
hair, wooden eyes and copper
hands. I almost forgot
that I wasn't a whole woman, and
the brown paper sack ripped,
yellow and purple fruit
beckoning me to chase.

# Combat Hunger

I didn't even know
where I was walking. The smell
of orange chicken woke me
out of my daze, but then I
remembered that I'm
on a diet, that I can never
be thin enough, and my mind
returns to a picture
of me in a blue dress,
me too wide next to two
tiny women. I see
a sign, *Combat Hunger.*
Was this sign
for me?

# In Line at Trader Joe's

a white-haired woman asked me
what day it was. *Thursday,*
*October 17,* I said. I didn't know
if she was testing my sanity
or hers, but she immediately
dropped her red plastic basket
behind the shelf with pumpkin
bars and chocolate-peanut butter
cups, covered her pink lips
with her grandmotherly hands and said
*Oh dear* as she blankly limped
out the store through the automatic
doors. I didn't know if I should
tell the cashier to stop
scanning my mango yogurts,
but I slipped my card
in the machine to pay, not knowing
if she forgot her son's birthday or
if she was late to book club or
happy hour, or if she needed
to pray at the cemetery before
the gates closed, and I couldn't
remember the last time
I replaced the flowers
on my dad's grave, and I
hit the glass doors
with my red cart as I
tried to remember where
I parked my car.

# Memory

The silence he cannot hear stings
his feet. He sits on a stool
in a bar, peeling the label from
a Stella Artois or maybe sipping whiskey
on the rocks, watching some game,
muted volume, picked by yesterday's
bartender. The seats near him
are empty, and he drains
his glass. He remembers
his toes intertwined
with his lover on top of
a mountain, sipping champagne after
hiking to the peak — to the spot
where he knew there was a purple
heart spray painted on the cliff-
side. She wasn't
the first woman he carried
over the creek on this trail.
He called this his church,
where he met God under
a 70-degree sun, where he
could see Matchbox cars below, but
he couldn't hear them. And he bowed
down to his lover's feet, memorizing
the flawless shape of her toes. But
he cannot remember her name.

# From My Porch

A green parrot perches on a power line.
Next door, a child shoots hoops in the alley,
tongue out as he tries to make a trick shot.
The bird, perhaps learning a new song, chirps
a few uncertain notes, shaking.

Tremendous twilight, wise, certain;
pink light illuminating the one cloud in the sky,
a gentle wind shaking the line,
shadow waning.
The parrot bounces, opens his beak.

The little boy jumps with his ball.
His mother calls out, dish towel in hand,
"Time for your bath!"
Is he really all that dirty?
He squints his eyes and jerks his arm
throwing the ball one last time.

They are the prudent ones.
He and the bird know that time will wait,
they can try again,
the song is perfect.
—Tomorrow is something to look forward to.

# Afternoon Tea

It hit me this afternoon that I am
40 — and a cliché. I bike to hot
yoga, sweat the toxins out. Slather
on Mary Kay night cream to keep my
wrinkles at bay. Call Nutrisystem when I have trouble
buttoning my pants. And I drink tea because my life is
cold, browse Pinterest to see what kind of art I can
create from the rectangle tea labels
instead of looking into my husband's
eyes. I try to mimic what the phrases suggest. And then
tattoo my skin with the tiny tags of wisdom on the end.

## Swallow

I didn't know love
looked like diamonds
branded on my back by the cold metal
balcony of a fire escape or that it smelled
like vomit and Bud Light or that it sounded like
the word no — two letters invisible in the winter sky.
Maybe love is
lines on liquor bottles that don't
stop me from drinking. I curl my hand
around a bottle of merlot and swallow
while a priest sprays holy water
in another city. *He* sips
communion, light shining
through stained glass windows
while I throw my wine bottle,
trying to crack the panes.

# Row 12, Seat A

I was a little drunk
after some chardonnay
at the airport bar where
I had slouched on a stool, legs
crossed, grading
essays in purple ink. Now,
on the plane, it was not
full, and there was an empty
seat between me and some
stranger. I didn't want to
flip through a magazine
found in the seat back pocket,
listen to top hits of the 1980s,
or chit-chat with my row-mate.
I wanted a moment in my
window seat to enjoy my rare
inebriation, to let my mind
sift through sand for rubies
in the extra gray-leather space. I
wanted to gaze out the window,
to dream of leaping
onto Mars where I would lay
in its red dust alone,
making dirt angels visible
by telescope before returning,
ready to sober up.
So when the stranger began
to speak, I fantasized
punching him in his chubby nose;
instead, I blabbered
about how my sister

is becoming my brother,
and how my mother won't
call him his preferred name.

# Message: Undeliverable

She wanted that house so badly that she
licked the door on the way out after she
viewed it: she thought her tongue would

seal the deal. She wanted it not just
for its stainless steel appliances, double
sinks or extra bedroom, not for the

closet cozy enough for a midday
nap. Not because most of her
furniture would fit just right and

she wouldn't have to paint the walls.
It wasn't the space but it was
the space — family games, movie nights,

joy. So when she heard another family
got the house instead, she knew it
was an omen. Maybe just

for the week, maybe for a thousand years. She
crawled back to her house, turned the oven on
and burned the chicken and broccoli casserole.

# I don't feel like a lady

Cloaked in French vanilla,
my ball gown crenellated lace—
     my feet bare.
I wear a crown of green leaves
white daisies woven in frizzed auburn hair,
     But my feet are bare and
     I don't feel like a lady.
My eyelids are
golden, my lips scarlet, cheeks a glass
of rosé spilled on ivory face,
     but I don't feel like a lady
I plié and pirouette
around the shadowy
forest. The darkness
creeps through
my soiled bare feet
on the scabby ground.
     I choose mud
over pointy shoes,
my toes free.

# Santa Barbara

She fell in love with a town
she couldn't live in. Narrow
streets, ocean on one side,

mountains on the other, a job
teasing her to come, the scent of jasmine
and tranquility. But she couldn't move

there. It understood her
as she drank its wine
and tongued its rich

chocolate truffles, watching
people who weren't
her neighbors, returning

to their postcard homes. This town stole
her soul. She traveled alone
but not alone, so she

couldn't stay. Face unwrinkled
but eyes of history,
hot rain dropped as her chest

rose and fell, rose and fell
uncold, memorizing the view
she would visit again

in the twilight moments of sleep.
And she ate apples instead of raspberries
that tasted like drinking champagne

with nothing to celebrate.

# The Black Dress

My body molded
to my bed,
long, brown hair fanned
behind me.

I sang hymns
in the house of God today.
I cooked a customary
Sunday roast beef,

and I wear a black dress.

My eyes are open windows,
letting the chill in,
and I ache to close them.
I stare at the blank ceiling,

in my black dress.

I shop for groceries,
scrub floors,
flip pancakes for the
children's breakfast.
That makes them happy,

while I wear a black dress.

My skin feels soft, sensual.
I contort my body
into triangle shapes —
become a warrior —

in yoga.
Now I lie motionless.

Beautiful in my black dress.

When I do cartwheels,
I will still wear
my black dress.

# Why doesn't she have any wrinkles on her face?

Maybe it's because she didn't spend enough time
with the wind battering her face

or she never
squinted while staring at the sun

and she didn't pause to think
about children dying in the streets

or maybe it's because her jaw
was sewn shut with flesh-colored thread

or maybe she couldn't find
the energy to be angry when her foot was stepped on again

or maybe birds didn't
spin round her head while she was asleep

> but it could be because
> she wears a mask

and on a rare day
when she lifts that mask

you see broken glass
embedded in her skin

and there's also a television screen
in her eyes playing back scenes from the war in which her
husband fought

and a map on her forehead
that has never been unfolded

or if you push her hair aside
next to her right ear

you might notice
a small tattoo of a lock with no key.

# Evening Tea

Walking with my cup of
chamomile down to the bay,
the stars begin to rise. I think about
slipping in the still  water, but I know it
isn't deep enough. God, how I hate the word
perfect. There's dog hair and  grass blades
all  over  my  floor, and  I can't  remember
the last time I changed the sheets. Make-up
hides my dark circles, and I'm unsure if my
crepe-paper hands are old or just dry
from the weather. Sipping my tea,
steam hits my face. The fog in
my eyes confuses me, so I
walk  back  home.

# 3

## Moonless Mexico

She lost the moon in Mexico
one Sunday night. As she sits
in a doctor's office
where she can't speak
the language, she touches
her neck and asks
for Klonopin.
Heavy wooden door,

stone walls, cross
above her bed... *I'm going to fucking
kill you, bitch*—he pinned
her down, squeezed her throat
slapped the side of her head. Collapsing,
shaking as he un-
clasped his hands
from her neck, and backed out of the room.
She was grateful the light
in the room was dim. Staring

blankly in the mirror, she drops
the tweezers down the drain,
trembling, as she tries
to reshape her eyes. Vomiting
on the freshly-hosed cobblestone street, she rubs
her shoulder. When she boards
the plane to return home, she can't help
but cry as she witnesses the tender touch
of a baby nursing from his mama,
tiny hands.

A restraining order is    just
a piece of paper; it is    not
as heavy as the    gun
he owns. How can she
protect    herself?
She tells her    children
she loves them    with an unsaid
goodbye at the end of every    whisper.

Hot, hot water. She rinses
the sweat, drenched
nightmares, grateful
she doesn't remember
all of them, but she
will never forget.
She pulls on her
pastel cats socks
her son picked out,
her only
morning comfort.

And when he slaps her, chokes her, she

screams
but not loud enough. She claws back but not

strong enough, she succumbs;
breath by breath by unbreathed breath.

A woman from the adjoining room

pounds. *It's Clare, from next door. Are you ok?*
She opens the door, reaching the knob from

the floor because she can't stand.

Fear keeps her silent, her jaw still sore.

She had a dream. When he banged on
her door, she sat

on the other side, and she
didn't open it. He never came

into her room that night. He never
strangled her or hit her.

The thought of dying
didn't enter her mind.

Back against the door,
she stared at the cross

over her bed, and she
trusted it to protect her.

He went away. She never
saw him again.

She throws a sweatshirt
on even though she's not
cold and super-glues
the broken dinosaur leg
on her son's toy —
needing to fix it,
just in case. *Good girl,
good girl,* he had repeated.
She never wanted to hear
those words again. She cut
the bruises from the apple
and decided never
to wear lace again.

The thing that gets her most
is his cocky walk and how
he flashes his straight,
white grin, as if his fingerprint
didn't live in her bones, while she stumbles
on a smooth sidewalk on her way
to her 8:30 a.m. Wednesday
therapy session. Maybe this is sad,
maybe it's not,  but she could

forgive him
if he shook
a little, if

he said I'm sorry
while looking straight
into her eyes. That
would help stitch open wounds,
but she knows she must pick up
the needle and thread it herself.

She dreamed once again. This time
she opened the heavy door because
she didn't know what was coming.

He threw her on the bed, and as he tried
to pin her down, her legs were
quick enough to kick him

off of her, sending him tumbling
on the cheap red carpet. His breath
fast and violent, he came at her again,

yelling, *I am going to fucking kill you,
bitch.* She shouted back *Nooooo*
and the power from her voice

filled her body and she shoved
him away. He threw his hands
in the air and quietly

left the room. She was able
to sleep without nightmares or
drenched sheets, she wasn't

afraid, she didn't need
therapy or Klonopin.
She felt whole.

*Horoscope 1-26-20: Trauma destroys your internal compass.*
*Healing reconstructs it.*

She blew an eyelash
off her fingertip, made
a silent wish which electrocuted
her whole hand. Her skin
was shiny when she stared
in the mirror, and she reached
deep into her make-up kit, touched the right
side of her neck and found
strength, all that was left, in her little toe.

## On Top of Crisp Sheets

Their bed lies beneath
a magnolia tree, blooming
each day, its canopy
spreading wider, casting
ghost-shaped shade, shielding
more sun every rotation of Earth. Her
head in the crook of his neck, she wishes
she was as obsessed with him as she
was about cottage cheese or clean
ears. She dreams about not giving
birth, and that the strip mall
hospital has no room for her,
and she fears that her belly
will stay swollen forever. She wakes,
apologizing for the drool on his chest.

## The Sweater

I slept with your shirt that you folded on your
pillow when you deployed, left with the faint
scent of moss, sandalwood and man, a smell uniquely
yours. I wear your sweater now,
the soft blue one, when it's
cool at night and I walk alone. This sweater,
bought when we moved into the drafty house
because you said your others
scratched your skin, now droops from my thin body.
But tonight I felt your breath on my neck,
tickling me, making me squirm.
Forgive me, I smiled in your sweater, stirred by you.

# Undone

When he died, he didn't
brew her coffee anymore.
She yelled at a him
not there. *How dare you leave me*
*without instructions!* Her fingers
didn't know which buttons to touch.
Should she add water
to the 8 or 10 mark on the pot? So she sat
on a swing in a park
next to the nearest
Dunkin' Donuts, staring
at the orange and pink sign, watching
customers cradle their steaming cups
as they left the shop. She
wasn't ready to go in and utter
her order – nothing fancy,
just a plain black coffee.
She didn't know
if she ever would be.
She pumped her legs
and let the cold Massachusetts
wind push her,
ever so gently.

# Copacetic

It drives my husband crazy,
the way he thinks I pick

eggs from a carton. Maybe it
looks like I'm blindfolded and grab

the first egg I touch, even
if it's in the middle of the dozen.

He likes order—pick the eggs
from front to back. I, too,

am methodical. First, the freckled
ones, or maybe the ones not

quite ovular. Sometimes I snatch
the runt of the litter or

the one a lighter shade of brown
than the others. Deciding

which egg will become part
of my recipe brings me back

to middle school, waiting
to be adopted on a P.E. basketball team,

selected last because I was short.
I want to live my life

finding beauty in the imperfect,

creating disorder wherever I go.

# I don't

My dress is heavy in September.
I'm wearing pain in the form
of organza, guilt
the color of blue.

I don't remember getting
dressed, but I know
you zipped me up.

Autumn was my
downfall, your gravelly
voice, the canyon,
you told me
you needed me. Butterflies
kissed my skin.

> I should have
> run, but I stayed.

And this dress is
so heavy, and although I long to be naked,
I don't
> Undress.

# Christina's World

*After Andrew Wyeth*

After he left,
she lost the use of
her feet, her legs,
as if her broken
heart spread down
to her limbs.
So she carried
her dead weight,
crawling. She wore
the belted pink dress,
the one which made his
head turn, and pushed her
dark hair back so it wouldn't
fall in her eyes. Creeping
through the field
of starving grass between
their farmhouses, she dragged
herself until she could see
his porch under the gray sky.
Love unreturned is still
love, after all. She waited,
willing him to notice her
figure on the part of his land that he
neglected. She could move
no longer, and as rain
began to fall the grass
kept browning, burning, despite
water quenching its thirst.

# Getting Dressed for the Ball

Sometimes the gaudy emerald and diamond
necklace you gave me is so tight it

becomes a noose and I can't breathe
until you unhook the platinum clasp

with your manicured fingers. Sometimes
the diamonds are so sharp that

they stab me, and I bleed
a blood the color of night.

The emeralds become onyx. Sometimes
the weight of the stones is so

heavy that they crush my
heart and disturb the rhythms of

my pulse. Sometimes, just
sometimes, they make me

realize I'm not as beautiful as I thought,
and I chop my hair off, leaving ragged edges.

# I Couldn't Sleep

Black circles under my eyes, I couldn't sleep.
"Why do you pace the floors all night?"
—Because I've made my husband drown
in gobs and heaps of spite.

I can't bury it. Body flailing,
his eyes wide, mouth gasping.
I stretch my arm to him, floating,
urge him closer, grasping.

I cry, coughing: "I didn't love
him like I do you. Please don't leave."
He grabs my hand—holding tight—
and says: "For some reason, I believe."

# Sunset

The scent of blown-out birthday candles
swoons over the city. As I walk
through the honeyed streets alone
in an oversized sweater, I become lost
in your life, how you use tomorrow
as an excuse, how you age
differently than me, how you must be
replanted every spring and how I die
to the ground at the end
of every season. You may bloom
longer, but I come back to life,
sniffing the air as if it was made
of lemons and limes. Sometimes I drown
in your frozen sea, and sometimes
I see a sonnet written in your blue
irises. I turn down my alley,
legs calm enough to lead me home.

Orange shouldn't fade into indigo,
but it does.

## On a Field, Sable, the Letter A, Gules

Her head beneath a darkened hood,
creeping quietly, parting air,
haunting the boulevards unseen—
always in moonlight, never in sun.
This town has been so cruel to her,
slamming doors and not whispering.
She tucks her beauty, eyes and heart
in pockets always empty now.
She wishes shame could be scrubbed off:
exfoliated with sugar,
rinsed down the drain.

# The Dream

I had a dream last night:
We left our house in San Diego

and moved to Philadelphia, to an old ranch home.
And this house had bathtubs with glass doors

lined one after the other in a long row
but all I could think about

was my old closet in my coastal home.
Oh, the shelving and the silver bar

with room for a thousand dresses — and the feeling
this unnamed space the closet afforded me—

the thrill of all that silk hanging,
organized by color.

# Ode to Pain

You come as a bee, stinging the
palm of my hand, inviting your friends
to do the same, multiplying. You are
the vomit that won't come after one too many
gin and tonics, leaving nothing behind

but pounding. Why wouldn't you just let me
expel your mess? Please, before I pass out. You
are everything behind the smile on my
unwrinkled face, in my burned throat,
scalded by reaching for sweet juice but chugging

vinegar. If only I had taken the time
to sniff you out, I wouldn't be so raw, so
red, so sore. I dove in too fast, you
deceiving me. Why is your color so
inviting, and why am I so stupid? Sometimes

I ask for you to come, but then I
am underwater, wrapped in seaweed, lungs
about to burst. You take the
air from me and you eat me up, as if
I am a ripe strawberry. Then you rip

my heart out and roll it down a hill. You spin
when I ask for affection, or just to be
fucked. You are the resounding, echoing
no. I feel you when I sit on the stoop,
head down, nobody stopping to ask to see

my eyes. You are what happens to me when I

wake up the day after surgery, and I haven't
had time to reach for the pill bottle. Maybe
I'll still feel you on my three small scars
when it rains outside. I don't know if

you're ever going away. I think I'll still
find you when I slip down the crevice
on a sunny hike, ankle scraped, maybe sprained.
Is my rescuer coming? I only see shadows
of birds circling overhead waiting

to peck me. The blood drips down
the rocks into the canyon below, maybe enough
for a coyote to sniff me out. The blackness
comes and I dream, and it's so unsettling. I see
dead people. My dad. Why does he

haunt me now? My mom is there, too,
although still alive, taunting me, placing
piles of stones in my pockets. I
take each stone out, read them as if
they are fortune cookies, and plop them

in a pile next to me. They all say your
name on them. Every last one. You
are just a word, a noun, sometimes
a verb. I read them all again,
heavy. Pain pain pain pain.

4

# March 19, 2003

Seven-pound dark-haired baby
nursing from my breast,

half drinking, half dreaming,
while I wonder if his dad

will ever hold him. Orange
and red raindrops fall from

the sky as I sit, not blinking,
in my brown chair. My husband

presses a black button with his thumb
from the back seat of his

jet, releases a missile
that kills an *enemy*,

a child? The distance from the cloud
to the ground is too great to

know what's ablaze. Is that fireball
heading for his plane? I try to breathe

but the air won't leave my lungs.
The two of us--new mother,

sleepy baby, bonded to this brown chair,
watching the world burn.

# Memory By Scent

Sitting under a pine tree
in the grass, my son plays
with a plastic sphere, trying to move
a tiny steel ball through a maze,
his tongue out
as he concentrates. A daughter
pushes her mother
in a wheelchair next to
the park, and they both
smile at us, the same
smile, from the same
face, one with deeper
wrinkles and wiser
eyes. I wonder if the mother
is from the memory care center
across the street and if a twilight
walk is their evening routine.
Their smiles tell me the story
of why the nursing home
was built next to a place
filled with the cracks
of baseball bats and children's
shrieks when they are caught
playing tag. I start
to count my son's
eyelashes, and I name
all five freckles on the right
side of his face. Without warning,
the lone pine smells like an entire forest.

# Lauren

I wanted to plop backwards in the
snow and wave my arms and legs
up and down, making a snow angel

next to you. I wanted to read *Where the Wild Things Are*
with a flashlight under a blanket fort
with you. I wanted to run with you

through a meadow, picking every dandelion,
blowing seeds in the wind.
I wanted to jump the waves, holding

your hand, while we looked for sand
dollars together. Instead, there was
blood, and somebody must have yanked

the bones from my body because I
crumpled into a lifeless heap of flesh on
the linoleum floor.

I swear I smell
baby powder. And a friend
left flowers on the porch.

# In His Own Room

I am certain
of three things:
he is warm, he is
breathing, he
is alive. But I am

too tired to know
any more—new mom
perched over his crib

not because I heard him
cry, but because
I didn't. Wrapped

in a blanket, he defines
peace. I lumber
back to bed, in search
of my own peace,
green eyes closed.

# Crosswalk

*Hector,* I overheard him
tell the paramedics while I

propped him up in the middle
of Sixth Avenue, his lip and head

bloody, surrounded by people
dropping their kids at school.

*Do you remember
what happened?* they asked him.

*Yes.* He told them he was
in the street, holding up his

stop sign, wearing his orange
safety vest, when the teenagers

hit him with their car. This
was a man I brought chocolate chip cookies

to once or twice a year and said
*thank you* or *have a nice day*

after he helped my sons and I
through the intersection, this man with his kind

smile missing a few teeth, weathered
skin, eyes shaped like peaches. I knew

him just enough to call him
my favorite crossing guard, but I

never thought to ask his name.

# Soaking

Lavender and chamomile fizzing
from bubbles, I'm staring

at the white tiles, rectangles,
figuring out their different

patterns. It reminds me
of hopscotch chalked on

pavement or a carefully crafted
cobblestone street. Who knew

there were so many shades
of white? Maybe it's just natural

variations, or it could be the lighting
in this room. Delicate water droplets

from the steamy bath may have
grayed the milky white, or my eyes

are playing tricks on me.
Maybe they're all the same.

I think about how I have to call
the school and let them know

my son is sick,
but it's all a lie. I wonder

how long I can sit here, skin
pruning, until the next thought

interrupts my peace.
I'm so thirsty.

# The Power of the Dragon

I found a dragon
in my purse. Wrinkled,
I wasn't sure if it was stuck
at the bottom of my black
and white bag for weeks
or months. Sharp teeth,
strong wings, scales
all down its back—
erasure marks inside
the legs, horns and tail,
and I imagine
my son trying to perfect
each detail. I can feel
his 9-year-old arms wrap
around me as I study
this art, and I clutch
his drawing to my chest
before sinking to the floor,
unable to move.

## Backwash

He walked slowly
in the middle of
painted lines on a
four-lane road —
palms facing down,
fingers fanned, dirty
blond hair days away
from being dreads, scraggly
beard a shade darker,
open flannel shirt, bird
chest that looked finely plucked—
near a yellow drive-thru
taco shop with red lettering
advertising their quesadillas
and burritos, and he was probably
the lead singer in a ska band,
or maybe a surfer; the air
smelled like
industrial glue as
light fell out of the sky
and I wondered if he
could taste my salted
bitterness and spice
as I continued driving
to soccer practice,
seat belt tightly buckled.

# Anxiety

I stare out of my office window
waiting for my tea to steep,
watching a woman sitting
on a red metal chair at a matching table,
her right leg furiously tapping while
my hair grays. My hair grays
while she listens to music
pumping through her ear buds—
piano notes to calm her or
maybe untamed guitar riffs
that mirror the bounce in her leg. She enjoys
the fresh air, her laptop lid closed,
while my hair grays and I
intrude in her life, if only
for a moment. My hair grays
while I think of my son
and how at age 16, he swallows
Prozac each night so he can
walk through the halls
of his high school, his eyes not
glued to the cheap linoleum floor.
I sip my tea and curl my long
strands around my index finger and decide
to pluck out every last gray.

# Mother Isn't Always Right

Three times, three times I asked
if you wanted a jacket before
we left for your brother's
soccer practice. *No,*
you insisted, and I, determined
to teach you a lesson, didn't
grab one for you. *He'll regret
that decision,* I thought. Sitting
on an old blanket, our hips
touched as you read your
picture book, and I read
poetry. You took my long, brown
hair and tucked it over
your lips, making a mustache,
and I started to see goosebumps
rise on your skin. You flipped
to another page before you admitted
that you were cold. I scooped
you onto my lap and covered
you with the clean side
of the blanket, warming you. You laughed
as I rubbed your little arms,
and I sucked that laugh out of the air,
into my lungs, and it tickled
my blood, and I placed your hand
over my heart so you could feel
how fast it was beating.

## Amen

I believe in the stillness of dawn. A gray sky,
starting to pink, in my overgrown garden,
jasmine drifting through the morn. Children
in bed, steam rising from apple tea. Breathe.
I don't want a God who causes me to
bruise. I want a Counselor who will
stop my skin from welting. Tomorrow
is the box I gift-wrapped my worries in. Today,
I write. Give me a now where my mind
dims down. Give me beliefs that are
light beams through my fingers for all to feel.

# Acknowledgements

The author would like to thank the following publications, in which these poems appeared, sometimes in different versions:

*The Write Launch:* "3 Otis Street"

*Adanna:* "Don't Send Me Flowers"

*Poached Hare:* "Morning Tea"

*Swimming with Elephants:* "Unbending," "Memory by Scent"

*Little Patuxent Review:* "For Some Reason"

*San Diego Poetry Annual:* "In Line at Trader Joe's"

*Westchester Review:* "Row 12, Seat A"

*Apeiron Review:* "Message: Undeliverable"

*The Road Not Taken:* "On a Field, Sable, the Letter A, Gules"

*Literary Mama:* "March 19, 2003"

*Prometheus Dreaming:* "Lauren"

*Hummingbird:* "Swallow," "The Power of the Dragon"

*Broad River Review:* "Backwash"

Joshua, Gabriel, Nicholas and Kellen, everything I do is for you. Dreams do come true! Thank you Keith for your support. Blas, your insight and honesty into my work are invaluable, but your friendship is the true treasure. Sandra, thank you for pushing me west when I was going north. Ilya, your patience and your genius are inspiring. Thank you to all the strong voices of the women poets that have had influence over my writing, including Ellen Doré Watson, Ellen Bass, Maya Angelou, Louise Glück, Sharon Olds, Emily Dickinson, Lucille Clifton, Anna Akhmatova, Victoria Chang, Sandra Alcosser, Malena Mörling, among many, many others. To my friends and family, you have sown many seeds in my life that bloom in vivid colors, and I appreciate all of your sunshine and water. And Iain, you are my happy place.

## About Atmosphere Press

Atmosphere Press is an independent, full-service publisher for excellent books in all genres and for all audiences. Learn more about what we do at atmospherepress.com.

We encourage you to check out some of Atmosphere's latest releases, which are available at Amazon.com and via order from your local bookstore:

*Big Man Small Europe*, poetry by Tristan Niskanen

*In the Cloakroom of Proper Musings*, a lyric narrative by Kristina Moriconi

*Lucid_Malware.zip*, poetry by Dylan Sonderman

*The Unordering of Days*, poetry by Jessica Palmer

*It's Not About You*, poetry by Daniel Casey

*A Dream of Wide Water*, poetry by Sharon Whitehill

*Radical Dances of the Ferocious Kind*, poetry by Tina Tru

*The Woods Hold Us*, poetry by Makani Speier-Brito

*My Cemetery Friends: A Garden of Encounters at Mount Saint Mary in Queens, New York*, nonfiction and poetry by Vincent J. Tomeo

*Report from the Sea of Moisture*, poetry by Stuart Jay Silverman

*The Enemy of Everything*, poetry by Michael Jones

*The Stargazers*, poetry by James McKee

*The Pretend Life*, poetry by Michelle Brooks

*Minnesota and Other Poems*, poetry by Daniel N. Nelson

*Interviews from the Last Days*, sci-fi poetry by Christina Loraine

*the oneness of Reality*, poetry by Brock Mehler

## About the Author

Betsy Littrell is a whimsical soccer mom to four boys as well as a writing instructor at San Diego State University, where she received her MFA in Creative Writing. When she's not writing (or when she is), she enjoys a good cup of tea, a glass of rosé and peaceful moments by the beach with a book in hand. Having grown up in Massachusetts, she is a superstitious Red Sox fan and also cheers for Liverpool soccer. Her work has appeared in several  journals, and this is her first full-length poetry collection.

CPSIA information can be obtained
at www.ICGtesting.com
Printed in the USA
BVHW031716231120
593969BV00005B/706

9 781649 219084